A STUDIO PRESS BOOK

First published in the UK in 2022 by Studio Press,
an imprint of Bonnier Books UK,
4th Floor, Victoria House, Bloomsbury Square,
London WC1B 4DA
Owned by Bonnier Books, Sveavägen 56, Stockholm, Sweden

www.bonnierbooks.co.uk

ISBN 978-1-80078-341-6

Written by Rachael Taylor
Edited by Ellie Rose
Designed by Maddox Philpot and Krissy Omandap
Picture Research by Paul Ashman
Production by Emma Kidd

A CIP catalogue record for this book
is available from the British Library

Printed and bound in China

The publisher would like to thank the following for supplying photos for this
book: Alamy, Getty, iStock, Mary Evans Picture Library and Shutterstock.
Every effort has been made to obtain permission to reproduce copyright material
but there may be cases where we have not been able to trace a copyright holder.
The publisher will be happy to correct any omissions in future printing.

TIFFANY & CO.

The Story Behind the Style

RACHAEL TAYLOR

Contents

ABOVE: A doorman stands outside a New York Tiffany & Co. store to greet customers.

An American Luxury Icon

Tiffany & Co. is one of the most famous brands on the planet. Its little blue boxes have become synonymous with romance and luxury, and, thanks to a dazzling performance by a young Audrey Hepburn, it's a household name. Yet, beyond the blue, diamonds and breakfasts, how much do you know about this icon of American luxury?

As you will discover, the origins of the brand stretch back to the 19th century and a young risk taker called Charles Lewis Tiffany. It was a time when important jewels had not yet been seen in America, but through well-timed deals and good-old-fashioned marketing, his vision to create the country's first luxury jewellery house came to life. The jeweller would go on to win over the rich and famous, with its most astounding pieces appearing regularly on red carpets to this day. Yet the iconoclastic views of its founder called on it to simultaneously cater to the mass market, allowing everyone to buy into the dream in some small way.

Tiffany & Co. might be a superbrand today, plastering its iconic robin-egg blue over billboards, perfume bottles and sunglasses, but at its heart the jeweller is an innovator. It was the creator of the modern solitaire engagement ring, an innovator in gemstones and publisher of the first-ever US mail-order catalogue. It has been a springboard for design talent, leading to jewellery icons such as the Bone Cuff and the playful Return to Tiffany heart-shaped locks, and even revolutionised the art of window displays. The story of Tiffany & Co. is so much more than its little blue boxes.

OPPOSITE: A Tiffany & Co. store in Hong Kong with an iconic blue window display.

The King of Diamonds: Charles Lewis Tiffany

Charles Lewis Tiffany, the man who would go on to win the moniker of New York's 'King of Diamonds', did not hail from a long line of jewellers. His start in life was more modest, making his ascent to high society all the more glittering.

Tiffany was born in 1812 to Comfort and Chloe Tiffany, and grew up in the small town of Killingly, Connecticut. The major business of the town was the production of cotton goods, and the family owned a manufacturing company. Tiffany was educated at local schools in the area before joining his father in the family cotton business.

By 1837, Tiffany felt restless. No longer satisfied by working at home with his family, he began to envision how he could make his own mark in business. He teamed up with a school friend, J. B. Young, and the duo set in motion a plan to open a stationery store in New York City. With a $1,000 loan from Comfort Tiffany, the ambitious 25-year-olds made the 150-mile journey south. The store, named Tiffany & Young, opened its doors at 259 Broadway that same year, and on its first day, $4.98 rang through the tills.

Tiffany & Young soon began to expand its remit, stocking glasswear, cutlery, porcelain, clocks and jewellery, and began to develop a

OPPOSITE: Tiffany & Co. founder Charles Lewis Tiffany, photographed by Jessie Tarbox Beals in 1902.

reputation as a purveyor of fine goods of taste. In 1841, the business expanded with the addition of a third partner, J. L. Ellis, and was renamed Tiffany, Young & Ellis. The trio expanded the store, doubling it in size by renting the adjacent unit, and continued to increase the quality of the goods they sold, with Young making buying trips to Europe to pick out English and Italian jewellery.

It was, in fact, political events in Europe that would be the making of this American luxury success story. In 1848, the status quo trembled as republican revolutionaries sought to topple European monarchies and strip aristocracies of their power and wealth. It was a societal upheaval known as the Springtime of Nations. More than 50 countries were impacted by this, but none more so than France, where the monarchy was overthrown and replaced with a republic. Such widespread panic and disruption had an impact on the price of diamonds, and Tiffany, Young & Ellis swooped. By now, the firm was manufacturing its own jewellery, and the opportunity to pick up diamonds at low prices put them at an advantage. The rocking of the aristocracy also loosened some important gems – the likes of which had never been seen in America before – and Tiffany secured a number of important heirlooms, including the collection of Hungary's Prince Esterházy.

In 1853, Young and Ellis decided to retire from the business, but Charles Lewis Tiffany was far from finished. He found new partners to work with, and the business was, at this point, renamed Tiffany & Company. Tiffany would go on to build his empire, grabbing headlines along the way. By the 1860s, the business was well established as an emporium of choice for the rich and the famous, both for its jewellery and its top-quality silver. In 1862, President Abraham Lincoln purchased a seed pearl necklace and earrings from Tiffany & Co. for his wife Mary Todd Lincoln, who wore them to her husband's inauguration ball.

In 1870, Tiffany & Co. moved into a large new store in New York's Union Square, marking the beginning of a major decade for the jeweller; one in which Charles Lewis Tiffany would earn the title the King of Diamonds. It was a single purchase that would truly jettison Tiffany into the high-jewellery stratosphere – a 287.42ct rough fancy yellow diamond. When cut and polished, what emerged was a diamond of staggeringly enormous proportions for a rare yellow diamond of that quality. It weighed 128.54ct and was named the Tiffany Diamond.

If the purchase of this now world-famous stone, which is on permanent display at Tiffany & Co.'s Fifth Avenue store in New York, signalled Tiffany's intentions to dominate the diamond market, his groundbreaking invention eight years later sealed the deal. Seeking to celebrate the beauty of diamonds, Tiffany designed an engagement ring in 1886 that remains a sought-after classic to this day. The Tiffany Setting engagement ring kicked back against the over-fussy designs of the time with a clean, minimalist band and a six-prong setting that lifted the diamond above the ring. The purpose for this innovative setting was to allow light to flow through the stone, and therefore maximise the sparkle. It was a huge hit, and the iconic design has become synonymous with engagement rings.

Just 15 years before his death, Tiffany pulled off a final coup. The aftermath of the French Revolution that had gifted Tiffany an abundance of important gems in 1848 and its early credibility in high-jewellery circles rumbled on. In 1887, the French government was masterminding a plan to sell the crown jewels of its fallen monarchy. Outwardly, it claimed that a democracy such as France had no need for "objects of luxury, devoid of usefulness and moral worth". The rumour mill suggested that it was in fact afraid of a power grab by Bourbons, Orleanists or Bonapartists, who might use ownership of the jewels to claim a right to rule. Tiffany cared little for this political posturing, but he did see an opportunity in it. He travelled to Paris to attend the auction of the French crown jewels at the Louvre. He sat in the audience, ready to make his bids, along with fellow jewellers, including a young Frédéric Boucheron, and Orleanists, members of the French royal family, whose pockets proved too shallow on the day to win back their family heirlooms.

When the final strike of the gavel fell, Charles Lewis Tiffany had in his possession close to a third of the historic crown jewels. He placed them in specially crafted red-leather boxes, embossed in gold with the words *Diamants de la Couronne*, translating from French as Crown Diamonds. Inside, impressed on the silk lining in the lid, was Tiffany & Co. New York and Paris, thus securing Tiffany & Co.'s place in the history books as a purveyor of royal jewels and his own coronation as the King of Diamonds.

BELOW:
A gold,
diamond and
enamel floral
brooch, made
by Tiffany & Co.
in 1890.

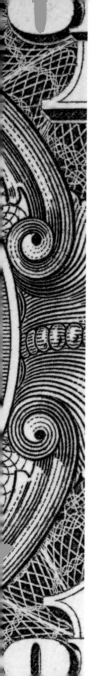

The Great Seal

In the early 1880s, the Great Seal, a steel engraving used to authenticate official US government documents, was starting to wear out and irregularities were appearing in the prints it created. Facing public pressure, and wary of the upcoming centennial of the seal, the Department of State set out to find a new engraver, settling on Tiffany & Co.

Accepting a $1,000 payment, the jeweller charged its head designer James Horton Whitehouse with creating the sketches. What he produced was a radical take on its predecessor. It offered a much more powerful-looking and detailed bald eagle clutching the symbolic 13 arrows, and an olive branch with 13 olives and leaves to represent the original number of US states.

Horton Whitehouse's seal was put into use in 1885. It lasted 17 years before it, too, had to be replaced due to wear. However, the design was so good that the Philadelphia firm Bailey Banks & Biddle, which won the new bid, were ordered to "furnish a fac-similie" of the Tiffany & Co. seal. The design was also used to decorate the US one-dollar bill, which remains in circulation today.

OPPOSITE: The seal design created by Tiffany & Co., as seen on a one-dollar bill.

Discovery and Innovation

As Tiffany & Co. carved out a market for itself as the first American luxury jeweller, it picked up some firsts along the way. Seeking to elevate its offering, it became the first US jeweller to adopt the British 925 standard for silver; making its silverware superior to others selling in the States at the time.

Also keen to acquire exclusive gemstones, the jeweller funded gem-hunting expeditions to far-flung exotic locations. Wholeheartedly marketing the discoveries of its gemmologists, the jeweller was responsible for introducing the world to tanzanite, kunzite and tsavorite garnets.

OPPOSITE: A silver wine jug made by Tiffany & Co. in 1890, which was gifted to a Thomas Horncastle Esquire by the Mutual Life Insurance Company of New York.

Tiffany & Co.
Jewelers Silversmiths

CHARLES II TANKARD, LONDON 1677, MAKER, T. R.
JAMES II TUMBLER CUPS, LONDON 1686, MAKER, J. S.
COMMONWEALTH WINE TASTER, LONDON 1649, MAKER, S.

Fine Old English Silver

Fifth Avenue & 37ᵀᴴ Street
New York

LONDON
44 New Bond Street

PARIS
7 Rue de la Paix

LEFT:
An advert for Tiffany & Co. silver that ran in collectors' magazine *The Connoisseur* in 1937.

BELOW:
A 19th-century afternoon tea with the Bridgham family, served from a Tiffany & Co. silver tea set.

A Silver Pioneer

One area of finery that Tiffany & Co. has long dominated is silverware. While the firm had traded in silver items since its inception, it was a partnership forged with leading New York silversmith John C. Moore that would elevate its efforts above the competition.

In 1851, the workshop started producing silver tableware, such as coffee pots and soup tureens, known as hollowware, exclusively for the jeweller. John C. Moore followed British silver standards, working with 925 sterling silver. With a purity level of 92.5 percent silver, it was more luxurious than other alternatives on the market. Tiffany & Co. became the first US jeweller to offer this silver standard, which would later be adopted across the country. As the relationship blossomed, Tiffany & Co. merged its own operations with that of the silver workshop. This merger also brought John C. Moore's son, Edward Moore, into the Tiffany & Co. family, who would prove to be a visionary.

For the next 40 years, Edward designed elaborate silverware for the jeweller that would win it international acclaim, including a prize at the 1867 Exposition Universelle in Paris. This made Tiffany & Co. the first American exhibitor to attract such an accolade for silver hollowware. His sources of inspiration were vast, and over the years his designs were influenced by everything from the Rococo style to Japanese lacquer and Islamic glass.

In the mid 19th century, there was a rapid expansion of wealth in the United States. As more families found riches, demand for Tiffany & Co.'s silverware skyrocketed. Keen to maintain its position as an industry leader at home and also drum up more business abroad – where American silversmiths did not command the same respect as their European counterparts – Tiffany & Co. started employing the best silversmiths emigrating from Europe. More international prizes followed, and many of the world's best museums have Tiffany & Co. silverware housed in permanent collections.

The style of Tiffany & Co. silverware has evolved throughout the decades but it remains an important part of the business. It still employs one of the largest groups of silversmiths in the United States, all hammering away at its workshop in Rhode Island in the shadow of many a mansion constructed in the Gilded Age when Tiffany & Co. silver was at its height.

BELOW:
A Tiffany & Co. silver-plated wooden paperweight calendar given to First Lady Jacqueline Kennedy from President John F. Kennedy to mark the Cuban Missile Crisis.

RIGHT:
An 1879 Tiffany
& Co. silver
coffee set with
gold, copper
and ivory
accents.

RIGHT:
Silver Tiffany
& Co. sugar
tongs with
the jeweller's
classic claw
motif.

ABOVE:
Smith & Wesson .44 Double-Action
Frontier Model Revolver decorated
by Tiffany & Co. in 1893.

ABOVE:
Smith and Wesson
.38 Caliber Double-
Action Revolver
with silver handle
made by Tiffany &
Co. in 1883.

New York Meets Wild West

Teapots and serving plates might be the first items that come to mind when you think of Tiffany & Co. silverware, but between 1880 and 1905 the jeweller produced some luxuriously decorated weapons.

The firm had long collaborated with the US military, creating medals and swords for its use, but its silver-handle guns were created for private clients with deep pockets. During this period, it would add embellishments to pistols and rifles made by American gun makers including Colt, Winchester and Smith & Wesson. In Tiffany & Co. workshops, the handles of the guns would be etched with decorative scenes, such as buffalo hunts and cowboys, or Art Nouveau flourishes. These high-art weapons would also be used to show off new techniques and rare materials, such as precious woods, ebony and the Japanese metal art of mokume.

Tiffany & Co. would often display these creations at world fairs, including the 1893 World's Columbian Exposition in Chicago and the 1900 Exposition Universelle in Paris, where they would come to represent a luxurious idealisation of the Western Frontier. Some examples can be found on display in The Metropolitan Museum of Art in New York today.

The Gem Hunter

By the time he was in his teens, in the late 1870s, New Yorker George Frederick Kunz was a serious rock hound. The self-taught gemmologist had amassed a collection of more than 4,000 minerals and gemstones, which he would go on to sell for $400 to the University of Minnesota, such was its quality. His fascination with rocks proved to be much more than a childhood hobby, and his collector's nose would lead him to ever greater treasures. One such find was an exceptional tourmaline. At the time, in 1876, coloured gemstones were a rarity in American jewellery collections, but Kunz thought he would try his luck by approaching Tiffany & Co. to see if the jeweller would purchase his tourmaline. Not only did it do so, it also gave the promising young gemmologist a job and would soon promote him to the role of vice-president at the young age of 23 years old.

Kunz made the discovery and acquisition of coloured gemstones for Tiffany & Co. a lifelong passion. As well as simply buying and selling gems, he was committed to educating others and took on roles as a lecturer and a curator, and was the author of many books and more than 300 articles on gems. The holy grail for any gemmologist is to discover a new gemstone. While Kunz might not have been out in the field when his moment came, his keen scientific brain ensured that he won that most coveted of accolades. In 1902, specimens of unidentified pink crystal had been unearthed in San Diego County, California. In search of an expert opinion, the miners sent samples to Kunz, who identified it as the mineral spodumene. However, spodumene had never been discovered in this shade of pink, making it a brand-new variety. The following year, his fellows in the gemmological community would name it in the Tiffany & Co. gemmologist's honour, calling it kunzite.

Another pink gemstone that Kunz had a hand in naming was morganite, the rose-coloured beryl discovered in Madagascar in 1910. At a meeting of the New York Academy of Sciences that year, Kunz suggested that the gem should be named after the famous financier J. P. Morgan in recognition of his support of the industry, and so morganite was agreed upon. Morgan was one of the most important gemstone collectors of the early 20th century, and had gifted many important stones to the American Museum of Natural History and Muséum National d'Histoire Naturelle in Paris. And who did he turn to for help amassing this gemmological treasure trove? George Frederick Kunz, of course.

Tanzanite and Tsavorite

Tiffany & Co.'s head gemmologist George Frederick Kunz passed away in 1932, but the fervour for coloured gems that he instilled in the jeweller would live on. The mid 20th century would yield yet more major discoveries. The first came in the 1960s, when an unusual colour-shifting blue-purple gemstone was discovered in the foothills of Mount Kilimanjaro in Tanzania. Legend has it that it was a Masai tribesman who first saw a cluster of the gems sticking out of the earth in 1967.

That tribesman is said to have brought his discovery to a local fortune hunter called Manuel d'Souza, who instantly registered mining claims in the hope that he had discovered a fresh sapphire deposit. Instead, it was a brand-new type of gemstone, and while there was much uncertainty as to what the gem was or what it might be worth, news of the discovery quickly spread and soon 90 additional claims were registered across a 20-mile area surrounding the discovery. Tiffany & Co. also got wind of this new gemstone and saw potential in it. Rather than be involved in the bun fight over mining rights, it established itself as the official distributor for the gem and, so, was given the right to name it. In honour of the country of origin, Tiffany & Co. dubbed it tanzanite.

In an advert introducing the gemstone in 1970, Tiffany & Co. displayed some gold, diamond and tanzanite rings made by its designer Donald Claflin over a black-and-white image of a safari scene. The accompanying text read, "From the

OPPOSITE: A rough tanzanite crystal that shows the gemstone's unique colour-changing properties.

foothills of Mt. Kilimanjaro comes Tanzanite, the loveliest blue gemstone discovered in over 2000 years. Tanzanite can be found in significant quantities in only two places in the world. In Tanzania. And Tiffany's."

At the same time Tiffany & Co. was busy promoting tanzanite in the US, another gemstone discovery was taking place back in Africa. This time, the find was made on the border of Tanzania and Kenya, near Tsavo National Park, and the gem was a green garnet. The discovery was made by Scottish gemmologist Campbell Bridges, who was employed by Tiffany & Co. as a consultant. It was, in fact, Bridges who had brought tanzanite to the US for the jeweller. Once again, Tiffany & Co. struck up a deal to be the exclusive distributor of this new gem. As such, naming

rights fell to Henry B. Platt, the jeweller's president at the time, who paid homage to the national park near its discovery by bestowing upon the gem the title of tsavorite.

In 1974, Tiffany & Co. ran an advert in *The New York Times* announcing the find to its customers. It told the adventurous tale of the tsavorite garnet's discovery, with a picture of Bridges and a giraffe in situ in Kenya. To describe this new gem, which is commonly referred to as simply tsavorite, the ad said it was "far more durable and far less expensive than emeralds".

ABOVE: A scattering of polished tsavorite garnet gemstones.

A Household Name

From the very beginnings of Tiffany & Co., back when Charles Lewis Tiffany was deal making with P. T. Barnum and courting Abraham Lincoln, marketing was always a top priority. After all, having the biggest diamonds, the world's best silversmiths or the most exciting coloured gemstones means little if nobody knows about it.

Over the decades, the jeweller has executed a brand-building exercise of epic proportions. It invented the modern engagement ring and created the world's most instantly recognisable brand colour. It ensured its jewels appeared on all the right stars, and even made Hollywood history. Tiffany & Co. has never stayed in the shadows.

OPPOSITE: The Tiffany & Co. sign outside its New York flagship store.

TIFFANY & Co.

Tiffany Blue

Only a few brands can be summed up in a single word or one standout product. For Tiffany & Co., it is a colour that has come to define the brand experience. Requiring little introduction, the shade that has become so intertwined with the American jeweller is a robin's egg blue hue with green undertones that gives it that instantly recognisable vibrancy. Tiffany & Co. has been using this shade of blue since the 19th century. A very similar shade to the one the brand uses now was selected as the colour for the front cover of its first Blue Book mail order catalogue in 1845.

Despite this fluctuation within the Blue Book, the iconic Tiffany Blue colour creeps into other early branding efforts, suggesting that it has long been associated with the jeweller. The jeweller's stand at the 1889 Paris World's Fair was decorated with swags of Tiffany Blue material. A gold, diamond and enamel orchid brooch, designed for Tiffany & Co. by G. Paulding Farnham in the late 19th century, can be found on display at The Metropolitan Museum of Art in New York in its original Tiffany Blue

OPPOSITE:
A display of blue boxes outside the Tiffany & Co. store on Avenue des Champs-Élysées in Paris.

RIGHT:
A pair of Pearls by the Yard earrings with a branded Tiffany & Co. pouch.

velvet jewellery box. As to why Charles Lewis Tiffany kept returning to this colour, the speculation is that it is reminiscent of the gemstone turquoise. This was a popular stone in the 19th century, and a wedding tradition at that time was for brides to gift their attendants a dove-shaped brooch carved out of turquoise as a thank you.

When the Tiffany Setting engagement ring – which was a huge hit on its launch in 1886 and remains a bestseller today – was first produced, it was packaged in a Tiffany Blue box. These covetable boxes became so popular that customers would try to buy empty ones. Tiffany & Co. made a point of refusing to do so, ensuring it maintained the exclusivity of the boxes. New York newspaper *The Evening Sun* reported in 1899, "Tiffany has one thing in stock that you cannot buy of him for as much money as you may offer… and that is one of his boxes." Tiffany & Co.

retorted that it was happy to give them away for free, as long as there was a purchased Tiffany jewel inside.

In 1998, Tiffany & Co. applied for, and won, a trademark for its famous brand colour, registering it as Tiffany Blue. It followed this up in 2001 by working with colour specialist Pantone to standardise the colour, which is notoriously difficult to make consistent across various mediums. On the Pantone spectrum the shade is named 1837 Blue in reference to the year the jeweller was founded.

OPPOSITE: The Tiffany & Co. store in the ION Orchard shopping mall in Singapore.

ABOVE: A Return to Tiffany necklace with a slick of Tiffany Blue enamel.

TIFFANY & CO.

TIFFANY & CO.

Believe In Love

Reimagining Engagement Rings

There is no jewel more iconic than a Tiffany & Co. diamond solitaire ring, and its presentation in a little blue box by a hopeful lover on bended knee has become synonymous with romance the world over.

While the classic Tiffany & Co. engagement ring might seem just that – classic – to the modern eye, its origin is one of radical reform. The ring, with its signature six-prong setting, first launched in 1886 and was like nothing that had been seen before.

At the time, engagement rings were a fussier affair. Elaborate engravings and ornate settings were popular, while diamonds and gemstones were set by pushing them into precious metals. This meant that only the tops of the stones were visible and little light could pass through – something that is essential for a diamond to emit the across-the-room sparkle we expect today. Charles Lewis Tiffany set out to revolutionise the 19th-century engagement ring. His design would set a single diamond high above the band, in a setting that allowed light to pass through it freely and therefore maximise its brilliance. Six simple gold claws held the solitaire in place to achieve this feat of precious acrobatics, while the band it sat upon was plain and smooth.

Tiffany believed nothing should distract from the beauty of the diamond. It was a striking minimalist masterpiece in a time of corsets, frills and bustles. Tiffany was so confident in his creation that he decided to bestow upon the ring his own name, and the design became known as the Tiffany Setting. With this, it is believed that Tiffany & Co. became

PREVIOUS:
An advert for
Tiffany & Co.
engagement rings
in the window
of its store in
Singapore's
Marina Bay
Sands mall.

TOP LEFT:
A window
display at a
Tiffany & Co.
store in Brussels,
Belgium.

BOTTOM LEFT:
A classic Tiffany
Setting diamond
engagement ring.

the first jewellery house to produce a signature engagement ring – a much-emulated tactic since.

The company then embarked on a dual-purpose marketing strategy that, again, challenged the status quo. While most jewellers of Tiffany & Co.'s stature were chasing important clients with one-off masterpieces, Tiffany had a vision in which his single design could appeal to both the elite and the more modestly heeled, simply by changing the size of the diamond. While there were clearly better margins to be made as the carat size increased, Tiffany decreed that all purchasers of the Tiffany Setting – no matter what size diamond they opted for – should be treated with the same respect and attention. He recognised that buying an engagement ring was an important milestone for couples, and that the sentiment did not dial up or down with the budget.

This democratisation of the luxury shopping experience, along with a superior sparkle, would go a long way to cementing Tiffany & Co.'s reputation as the go-to engagement ring jeweller.

More than 135 years later, the Tiffany Setting remains a bestselling, iconic design – and even the blueprint for the famous diamond-ring emoji. It has become so synonymous with engagement rings that many jewellers offer a similar style, just without the blue box. In fact, the term Tiffany Setting has become almost a technical description among professionals. This term is best kept out of marketing blurbs, however, as American big-box retailer Costco discovered in 2013 when Tiffany & Co. took it to court for trademark infringement after it described a ring it was selling as having 'a Tiffany setting'.

The enduring and steadfast appeal of the Tiffany Setting was captured wonderfully – and wittily – in a 2012 advert created by Tiffany & Co. Against its trademark blue background, it showed four identical rings captioned 1886, 1944, 1968 and 2012 with the tagline, What They're Wearing This Year.

Tiffany's engagement ring offering has widened over the years. The Soleste loops the central stone with halos of smaller diamonds. Harmony has a curvaceous band that is designed to fit snugly with a matching wedding band. Novo reduces the number of prongs securing the diamond to four for a more contemporary look. True brings the diamond closer to the band with a basket setting inspired by the initial T.

One of the most recent Tiffany & Co. engagement ring collections to launch is the Charles Tiffany Setting. These titanium or platinum rings set with solitaire diamonds certainly live up to the name, chiming well with the provocative spirit of the brand's first creation as the house's – and perhaps the world's – first line of engagement rings designed exclusively for men.

Breakfast at Tiffany's

One of the seminal moments in Tiffany & Co.'s branding history came in the form of Audrey Hepburn in a black evening dress and costume jewels, gazing dreamily into the windows of its New York flagship store, paper bag of breakfast in hand. This iconic

OPPOSITE: A romantic call to action at Tiffany & Co.'s store in Brussels, Belgium.

Hollywood moment was the opening scene of the 1961 film *Breakfast at Tiffany's*, inspired by the Truman Capote novella of the same name. As 40 guards and store staff stood to attention to protect the very real jewels within, Tiffany & Co. entered movie history.

As well as filming the opening scene on site, the crew returned to shoot within the store as the main characters, the eccentric café society girl Holly Golightly, played by Hepburn, and the struggling writer Paul Varjak, a role taken by George Peppard, do some shopping.

The central message of the film regarding its connection with Tiffany & Co. is that the store was a place of luxurious refuge where "nothing very bad could happen to you", as Holly Golightly put it in one scene. There's also an aspirational message. "I'm just crazy about Tiffany's", Golightly yelps, and speaks of planning to have breakfast inside the store one day once she's achieved fame and fortune. Crucial to cementing its mass-market appeal, Tiffany & Co. was also portrayed as an emporium that had something for everyone, as demonstrated when Golightly and Varjak go shopping on a $10 budget.

Though Tiffany & Co. had an invaluable amount of screen time and mentions in the script, Hepburn didn't wear any of its jewels in the movie. The closest she came was in a publicity shoot between takes when Tiffany & Co. boss Henry B. Platt was photographed helping her to try on the necklace Jean Schlumberger designed around the 128.54ct fancy yellow Tiffany Diamond. Though not worn, the necklace does appear in the film, stopping Golightly in her

OPPOSITE: A publicity shot for the 1961 film *Breakfast at Tiffany's*, starring Audrey Hepburn.

"When I get the [mean reds], the only thing that does any good is to jump in a cab and go to Tiffany's. It calms me down right away, the quietness and the proud look of it; nothing very bad could happen to you there. If I could find a real-life place that made me feel like Tiffany's then I'd buy some furniture and give the cat a name."

Holly Golightly in *Breakfast at Tiffany's*

LEFT:
A Tiffany & Co. bag shot in the Barcelona store, where a framed picture of Audrey Hepburn hangs on the wall.

OPPOSITE:
Breakfast at Tiffany's stars George Peppard and Audrey Hepburn.

tracks as she browses in the store, with the camera swooping in as she says, "It isn't that I give a hoot about jewellery, except diamonds of course... like that."

The Blue Book

The annual unveiling of the Tiffany & Co. Blue Book is a sparkling affair, for more than one reason. As well as the glittering jewels within the pages of this revered and glossy tome, there are also the glitterati that flock to the launch events it inspires. As much a collection as a publication, the Blue Book represents the best of the American jeweller through one-of-a-kind pieces of high jewellery that show off impeccable craftsmanship, atelier advances and the largest or rarest gems in its possession. It will offer up jewels that have taken years to bring to fruition, sometimes accompanied by specially crafted precious boxes.

To publicise these special jewels, Tiffany & Co. throws a lavish gala in New York attended by A-list celebrity guests, who will often wear pieces from the Blue Book as they pose for the cameras. The jewels will then go on tour, being presented at locations across the globe – and at yet more parties – as they seek out collectors with pockets deep enough to buy them. This is a strategy most luxury jewellery houses employ when creating and selling high jewellery.

While the methods Tiffany & Co. uses today might not be revolutionary, the first iteration of the Blue Book certainly was. The first edition was printed in 1845. Back then, it was given the slightly less catchy title of: Catalogue of Useful and Fancy Articles, Imported by Tiffany, Young & Ellis. Its function was that of any catalogue – to showcase goods it had for sale – but by posting it out to customers, Tiffany & Co. effectively invented the first direct mail catalogue in US history.

While the term 'mail order catalogue' might not instantly drum up visions of luxury today, in 1845 its purpose was not to hawk cheap items to a mass audience. Rather, it was to trumpet the arrival of Tiffany & Co.'s biggest coup to date – jewels and diamonds liberated from European aristocrats fallen on hard times. And the Blue Book has remained a beacon of taste and opulence ever since.

OPPOSITE: Actress Jessica Biel attends the Tiffany & Co. Blue Book 2016 gala in New York.

OPPOSITE
TOP LEFT:
Actresses Claire
Danes, Ruth
Negga, Reese
Witherspoon and
Haley Bennett at
the Tiffany & Co.
Blue Book 2017
gala in New York.

OPPOSITE
BOTTOM LEFT:
Lady Gaga wears
jewels from the
Tiffany & Co. Blue
Book collection to
the Annual Screen
Actors Guild
Awards 2019 in
Los Angeles.

ABOVE: Diane
Kruger attends
the Tiffany &
Co. 2016 Blue
Book gala in
New York.

Red-Carpet Rocks

Tiffany & Co. has a long history of dressing stars of the moment for the red carpet, and you will regularly spot its diamonds sparkling under the flashbulbs at events such as the Met Gala, the Oscars and Cannes Film Festival. Notable moments include Lady Gaga donning more than $5 million-worth of Tiffany & Co. jewels to the 2019 Golden Globes; only to trump herself later that year by wearing the Tiffany Diamond necklace to the Oscars, which is worth a reported $30 million and makes it the most expensive jewel ever worn on a red carpet.

With style writers poring over every look, ready to report back on who wore what, getting a celebrity to wear your jewels on a red carpet can deliver huge exposure and secure a brand's aspirational status. As such, this has often become more business transaction than friendly loan. It was reported that in 2011, Anne Hathaway was paid $750,000 for the pleasure of wearing a selection of Tiffany & Co. jewels as she hosted the Oscars.

LEFT: Charlize Theron in a Tiffany T diamond necklace at the British Academy Film Awards 2020 in London.

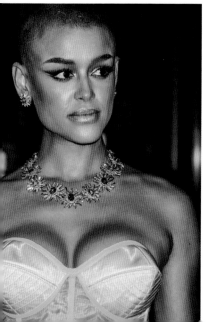

TOP LEFT: Gillian Anderson
wears Tiffany & Co. to the
British Academy Film Awards
2020 in London.

TOP RIGHT: Emma Raducanu
in Tiffany & Co. diamonds at
the *No Time to Die* premiere in
London in 2021.

LEFT: Jordan Alexander wears
Daisy jewels designed by Jean
Schlumberger for Tiffany & Co.
to the Met Gala 2021.

Tiffany and Diamonds

While Tiffany & Co. has garnered a reputation for curating a cornucopia of exciting gemstones from all over the world, there is one, above all, it is famed for – the diamond. After all, this is the jeweller whose founder was branded the King of Diamonds.

Tiffany & Co.'s association with diamonds started with the acquisition of important stones secured from fallen aristocratic families in the 19th century, and would be further bolstered by its acquisition of the Tiffany Diamond and invention of the modern solitaire engagement ring. Diamonds are a huge part of its business, but where do they come from today?

PREVIOUS: Kendall Jenner wears a Tiffany & Co. suite of jewels to the Met Gala in 2019.

OPPOSITE: Tiffany & Co. has built up a legendary reputation as a purveyor of the world's finest diamonds.

The Tiffany Diamond

In the heat of a South African diamond mine known as Kimberley, or Big Hole due to the depth of excavation (240m down by way of pickaxes and shovels), a momentous discovery was made in 1877. Miners liberated from rock a 287.42ct yellow diamond – an extraordinarily rare find.

Charles Lewis Tiffany heard tell of this discovery and did some deep digging of his own to pay $18,000 to secure the stone. Knowing how important this gem could be to his legacy, Tiffany sent his chief gemmologist George Frederick Kunz to Paris to oversee the cutting of the rough diamond. It was a task that would occupy Kunz for a year. The stone was cut and polished in a way that would maximise its vivid yellow colour, rather than achieve the largest carat size. As such, what resulted once the intricate process was complete was a 128.54ct cushion-cut stone with 82 facets – more than the traditional 58 facets on a round-brilliant diamond. Famous diamonds are usually given names, and for this gem, Tiffany had one in mind – his own, a move that would go some way to winning him the King of Diamonds title.

The Tiffany Diamond returned to the United States but rather than sell it, Tiffany decided to keep it and display it for all to see at Tiffany & Co.'s New York store, where it remains to this day.

Though the Tiffany Diamond has been in existence for more than 145 years, it has only been worn by four women. The first was socialite Mary Whitehouse, who borrowed the gem – at the time mounted in a white diamond necklace – for the Tiffany Ball, a fundraiser in Newport, Rhode Island, in 1957. Next came Audrey Hepburn, who slipped it on between scenes while filming *Breakfast at Tiffany's*. The diamond was now set in an elaborate ribbon-like necklace of yellow gold and diamonds created by French jewellery designer Jean Schlumberger. To celebrate the opening of a retrospective exhibition on Schlumberger's life and work at Musée des Arts Décoratifs in 1995, the Tiffany Diamond was transformed again. It was set into one of the designer's most iconic brooch designs, A Bird on a Rock, with a gold and diamond bird perched on top of this magnificent gem.

In 2012, to mark the jeweller's 175th anniversary, the Tiffany Diamond had another revamp, set in a contemporary platinum necklace accented with 559 white diamonds. This is the necklace that Lady Gaga would wear to the Oscars in 2019, and that Beyoncé wore in an advertising campaign for Tiffany & Co. alongside her husband Jay-Z in 2021.

LEFT: Lady Gaga wearing the Tiffany Diamond to the Academy Awards in 2019.

The 21st-century superstars both wore the famous gem while wearing long black dresses and their hair in an up-do in homage to Audrey Hepburn in *Breakfast at Tiffany's*.

A Diamond's Journey

The journey of a Tiffany & Co. diamond, big or small, started millions of years ago when intense heat and pressure at least 100 miles beneath the earth's surface transformed carbon to diamond. Major shifts in the earth, such as volcanic eruptions, brought these natural treasures ever closer to the surface, in reach of miners. There are many places in the world where diamonds can be found, and Tiffany & Co. sources from many of them: Canada, Russia, Sierra Leone, Brazil, Namibia, South Africa, Lesotho, Botswana, Tanzania and Australia. When the diamonds are extracted from mines, they are referred to as rough diamonds. These rocks must pass through the hands of many skilled sorters, cutters and polishers before achieving the sparkle you see in a boutique window.

Tiffany & Co. claims to have such exacting standards that it will only accept 0.04 percent of the world's gem-quality diamonds (a term referring to gems good enough to be placed in jewels – the less beautiful are destined for industrial work, such as the tips of drills). This puts the pressure on the sorters, whose job it is to evaluate rough diamonds and select the highest quality. The chosen few are then sent to Antwerp, the home of Tiffany & Co.'s diamond operation, and indeed a global centre for diamond cutting. The rough stones will then be individually assessed by gemmologists to determine which cut will produce the most

LEFT:
Tiffany & Co. buys rough diamonds from producers across the world.

beautiful diamond; carat weight will often be sacrificed
to achieve a gem with a superior sparkle. The weight of a
diamond is measured in carats, with one carat the equivalent
of 200 milligrams.

With a destiny mapped out, the cutting and polishing
process will begin, either in Belgium or at another of its
facilities in Botswana, Mauritius, Vietnam or Cambodia.
The art of perfecting diamonds is a hugely skilled job
that requires years of training. Once the stones are ready,
the majority are sent to the United States to be set into
jewellery. It is estimated that 16 million diamonds pass
through the Tiffany Jewellery Workshop and Gemmological
Laboratory in Pelham, New York, every single year.

OPPOSITE:
The Diavik diamond mine in Canada, operated by miner Rio Tinto.

TOP RIGHT:
Rough diamonds as they appear when first mined.

MIDDLE:
Diamond sorters must evaluate the stones to assess them for colour and clarity before they are cut and polished.

BOTTOM RIGHT:
A selection of yellow diamonds on display at a Tiffany & Co. store in Kuala Lumpur, Malaysia.

Tiffany Yellow Diamonds

Designers of Note

Tiffany & Co. has a history of celebrating and naming its designers, rather than secreting them away in the workshop to hide behind a brand name, as many luxury jewellery houses do. Often when running advertisements in newspapers, it would place a designer's name alongside its own when promoting jewels, and the most iconic designs will have the creators' names woven into the title.

Many designers have passed through the American jeweller, each leaving their own distinct mark on collections, but a few excelled to become forever synonymous with the house.

OPPOSITE: Tiffany & Co. president Henry Platt and designer Elsa Peretti outside the New York store in 1978.

Jean Schlumberger

Jean Schlumberger was born in 1907 in Mulhouse, a now-French town on the borders of France, Switzerland and Germany. His family was affluent and involved in textile manufacturing; a business they hoped to lure him into, but Schlumberger had other ideas. With a passion for art and a talent for sketching, Schlumberger sought out kindred spirits in Paris when he was in his 20s. He started by working for a publishing company and soon found himself at the centre of the Surrealist movement.

One Surrealist luminary in the fashion world in the 1930s was Elsa Schiaparelli, who asked Schlumberger to create some buttons for her. Impressed by his artistic vision, she would go on to commission him to create jewels and objets d'art for her label, which he did, incorporating wild motifs from harlequins to ostriches. Others would soon seek out his surrealist take on jewels, including legendary editor Diana Vreeland, who owned many of his pieces. The outbreak of World War II led to a pause in Schlumberger's creativity, as he fought with the French Army and the Resistance's Free French Forces, including surviving the Battle of Dunkirk in 1940. When war was over, Schlumberger returned to designing but did so with a fresh start in New York City.

In 1946, Schlumberger opened his own salon in the city with business partner Nicolas Bongard. A decade later, he would be approached by Tiffany & Co. president Walter Hoving who asked him to lend his talents to the American jeweller. He agreed, and a studio was set up for him at Tiffany & Co. with the gem vaults put at his disposal.

Schlumberger would make good use of the studio right up until his retirement in the 1970s. During this time,

he created many masterpieces, including resetting the legendary Tiffany Diamond in a ribbon-inspired necklace. Other iconic designs of his include those carrying his softly curving X motif, such as his Croisillon gold and enamel bangles beloved by Jackie Kennedy, and his Bird on a Rock brooches that perched precious birds atop large coloured gemstones. He was known for incorporating flora and fauna into his work, but did so with a surrealist edge to give it his unique Schlumberger touch.

OPPOSITE:
Former US First
Lady Jackie Kennedy
wearing two Jean
Schlumberger bracelets
in Newport, Virginia
in 1967.

ABOVE:
A gem-set Jasmin
necklace designed by
Jean Schlumberger
and made by Tiffany
& Co. in 1973.

BOTTOM LEFT:
The Tiffany Diamond
was set in a Jean
Schlumberger Bird on a
Rock brooch in 1995.

Elsa Peretti

Elsa Peretti was born in Florence, Italy, in 1940. Her family was wealthy, having made its money in oil, but the free-spirited Peretti would choose a different path – one that would lead her to be estranged from her family for much of her life. After a spell teaching French and skiing in a Swiss mountain resort, Peretti moved to Rome to study interior design and later took a job with Milanese architect Dado Torrigiani. In 1964, she reinvented herself once more, moving to Barcelona in Spain to work as a model. On the advice of her agency, Wilhelmina Models, Peretti moved to New York to further her career.

Beautiful, elegant and wild, Peretti soon became a poster girl for the hedonistic 1970s disco scene. She was a regular at infamous club Studio 54, partying with the likes of Andy Warhol, Cher and Liza Minelli, as well as fashion designer Roy Halston Frowick, known simply as Halston, who would prove to be an important influence in her life. Peretti started modelling for Halston but soon expanded her remit at the fashion brand to designing its jewellery collections in 1971. She had already been designing jewels for a couple of years prior to this, and her trademark was sensuous silhouettes crafted in silver, including a tiny vase on a leather thong.

At the time, silver was seen as a cheap, passé metal, but with the help of a few celebrity friends, Peretti overhauled its image. This led her to major award wins and a Peretti boutique in Bloomingdales. Tiffany & Co. was watching from the sidelines, and in 1974 it approached her to design

OPPOSITE: Elsa Peretti photographed walking along a street in New York.

70

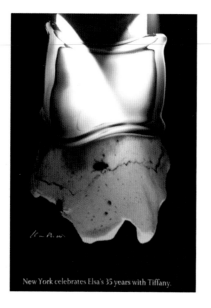

New York celebrates Elsa's 35 years with Tiffany.

ABOVE:
South Sea pearl and diamond earrings designed by Elsa Peretti for Tiffany & Co., c.1996.

BOTTOM LEFT:
An artwork hung at a party in New York in 2009 to celebrate 35 years of Elsa Peretti collaborating with Tiffany & Co.

a silver jewellery collection – a metal the jeweller had not worked with in its jewellery collections for 25 years at that point. Peretti would go on to win Tiffany & Co. a younger, more fashionable clientele, as well as creating style icons and delivering serious commercial success; at one point, it is estimated that her designs accounted for as much as 10 percent of Tiffany & Co.'s annual sales.

> "Touch is important: I get lots of my inspiration from tactile things."
> **Elsa Peretti**

Her many successes, later crafted in gold as well as silver, included sleek fava bean-inspired Bean designs, the provocative Bone Cuff designed to accentuate wrist bones, and a sensual Open Heart motif. Her strikingly simple yet versatile Diamonds by the Yard line of precious chain interspersed with diamonds is a steady hit, simultaneously selling for hundreds of dollars and tens of thousands of dollars, depending on length and carat count. In recognition of her contribution to the house, Tiffany & Co. renewed Peretti's contract in 2012 for another 20 years, paying a reported $47 million upfront. Sadly, the designer would not live to fulfil it, passing away in 2021, but her designs – and her name – live on at Tiffany & Co.

Paloma Picasso

Paloma Picasso was born in 1949 in Vallauris on the French Riviera, and delivered straight into a world of art and design. As the daughter of famous artist Pablo Picasso and painter Françoise Gilot, her destiny to join the creative arts seemed predetermined. Picasso's first interaction with jewels came in Paris in 1968 when she was working as a costume designer. Encouraged by a positive reception to necklaces she had designed using flea-market rhinestones, she began to study jewellery design. A year later, she presented her first serious works to a friend, the legendary fashion designer Yves Saint Laurent, whose response was to commission her to design accessories for one of his collections.

After a short period working for Greek jeweller Zolotas, Picasso moved to New York to take up a new job with Tiffany & Co., debuting her first collection in 1980. The jewels used large cuts of semi-precious gemstones, but treated them as seriously as if they were great luxuries. When asked why she worked with these gems, which at the time were seen as cheap alternatives to more upmarket diamonds, rubies, emeralds and blue sapphires, Picasso explained that she approached jewellery design like a painter and as such was drawn to the big swathes of bold colour these gems afforded.

Picasso's work for Tiffany & Co. was one of two halves: her work with big, colourful stones and then later her minimalist metal designs. Taking inspiration from the graffiti that surrounded her in New York, she created Scribble, energetic flicks of gold or silver that could be used as earrings, brooches or pendants. She would follow up with linguistic messages with precious metal spelling out 'Love', 'Oui', 'Kiss' and even a hashtag symbol. Other popular collections include the interlocking bands of Paloma's Melody that combine five connected bangles to create a single design. Olive Leaf, meanwhile, uses a leaf motif to create delicate designs inspired by the olive grove in the

garden of her home in Marrakesh, where she continues to design for Tiffany & Co. after more than 40 years with the house.

"My purpose in life is to make everything more beautiful."

Paloma Picasso

OPPOSITE:
Paloma Picasso is
known for working
with large cuts of
coloured gemstones.

TOP LEFT:
Paloma Picasso
introduces her first
collection for Tiffany
& Co. at its store in
New York in 1980.

BOTTOM LEFT:
Maria Sharapova
playing at the
Australian Open in
2010, wearing jewels
designed by Paloma
Picasso for Tiffany
& Co.

More Designers of Note

Tiffany & Co. has worked with many more designers throughout its history, each lending creativity and vision to the jeweller at different periods of its evolution. Donald Claflin, for example, who would later design for Bulgari, was a leading light at Tiffany & Co. in the 1960s. He created bold, colourful jewels, and playful, characterful brooches. Architect Frank Gehry brought an industrial edge to the jeweller in the Noughties, with tough-looking white-metal jewels, as well as his softer Fish designs that used tactile cuts of precious metal, hardstones and exotic wood.

This century has seen the installation of two high-profile creative directors at Tiffany & Co., both of whom shaped the direction of the brand through influencing its marketing efforts, overseeing new additions to heritage collections, as well as pioneering a few of their own. When Francesca Amfitheatrof joined Tiffany & Co. in 2014, it was a landmark moment. Not only had the role been left unfilled for five years before she arrived, Amfitheatrof would also be the company's first female design director.

Amfitheatrof was an artsy choice, and a sophisticated global citizen. She grew up in New York, Moscow, Tokyo and Rome as the daughter of an Italian mother who worked in luxury fashion PR and a Russian-American father who was a bureau chief at *Time Magazine*. She studied extensively in London, taking courses at Chelsea College of Arts, Central Saint Martins and the Royal College of Art, and not long after graduating, her first silverware collection was exhibited by art impresario Jay Jopling at his White Cube Gallery.

OPPOSITE: Francesca Amfitheatrof poses for photographers at the Tiffany & Co. Blue Book gala in New York in 2016.

PREVIOUS:
A mouse on a sled
holds a gold and
diamond Paper
Flowers ring
designed by Reed
Krakoff for Tiffany
& Co.

LEFT:
Reed Krakoff at a
Tiffany & Co. men's
jewellery launch in
Los Angeles in 2019.

Her first collection for Tiffany & Co. would prove to be
a strong one – Tiffany T. Playing with the first letter of
the brand's name, as Tiffany creative director John Loring
previously did in the 1980s when he introduced a block
motif T pattern, Amfithreatrof would use it most notably to
tail-end open cuffs. These remain a cult classic among the
fashionable. Throughout her three-and-a-half years with the
jeweller, Amfithreatrof would steadily bring innovation.

She spearheaded fresh commercial collections, created a brand partnership between Tiffany & Co. and fashionable store Dover Street Market, and elevated the Blue Book designs with three collections that made Tiffany & Co. a serious player in contemporary *haute joaillerie* circles.

Amfithreatrof's curtain call as she left Tiffany & Co. in 2017 – she would go on to head up Louis Vuitton's watch and jewellery division a year later – was also a zinger. Inspired by the urban landscape of New York and, more notably, a Tiffany & Co. Ball and Chain bracelet designed by Donald Claflin in 1971, she created the much-loved HardWear collection.

Next up was Reed Krakoff, who was given a newly created role of chief artistic director in 2017. Krakoff was an American fashion designer who had spent 17 years as the creative director at handbag brand Coach and briefly set up his own label.

Krakoff's first collection was titled Paper Flowers, inspired by its namesake but realised in precious materials. Lavish Blue Book creations followed too, and a revamping of Tiffany T with the T1 collection that played with knife-edge flourish on Tiffany & Co. engagement ring bands. He would carry this motif through to Tiffany True – marking the house's first new engagement ring design in more than a decade – which secretes the T motif in the setting of the diamond.

His other coup, much mocked in the press but ultimately iconic, was his line of Everyday Objects – items such as tin cans, protractors and LEGO-style building blocks all crafted in silver with price tags to match.

The Icons

A jewellery house does not reach iconic status through exquisite one-off high-jewellery creations alone; no matter how record-breakingly lavish they might be. In order to achieve truly legendary status, a house must also create jewels that are instantly recognisable at dinner parties and on social media. Designs that can be sold in the thousands and coveted by all.

With a long history of successfully creating for the mass market while simultaneously catering to the rich, Tiffany & Co. has excelled at this. The evergreen allure of many of its bestselling pieces has led to a steadily growing archive rich with jewellery icons.

OPPOSITE: A billboard in Xintiandi, Shanghai, showing the iconic Tiffany Setting engagement ring.

Tiffany Setting

Revered as the ultimate engagement ring – so much so that it was the basis for the ring emoji on all smartphones – the Tiffany Setting looks as chic and modern today as it did when it was first designed by Charles Lewis Tiffany in 1886. The Tiffany Setting can be identified by its minimalist band, with knife-edge detailing, and its trademark six-claw setting holding a single round-brilliant diamond. The claws are used to hoist the diamond above the ring, allowing as much light as possible to flow through it, which makes for a brilliant across-the-room sparkle. It was this innovation that made it stand out in 19th-century New York, and one that has kept it in style ever since.

Though the design has become standard issue throughout the jewellery world, the ring remains one of Tiffany & Co.'s bestsellers, despite carrying a significant premium compared to comparable imposters. One can only imagine that the lure of the little Blue Box it is sold in has something to do with it.

LEFT:
A Tiffany &
Co. diamond
Tiffany Setting
engagement ring,
and diamond line
bracelet.

Return to Tiffany

Return to Tiffany started out not as a jewel but as a keyring with a novel concept. First released in 1966, the gold or silver keyrings were engraved with the message 'Please Return to Tiffany & Co. New York' and a unique registration number. That way, if a set of keys were lost, they could be handed in to a Tiffany & Co. boutique and the number would be used to locate their owner.

The heart- and oval-shaped tags were a hit, and soon became an iconic purchase for Tiffany & Co. fans. Tapping into this, the design team extended the tags' remit to jewels in 1980, placing a 14ct gold heart-shaped tag on a box-chain necklace. Since then, the Return to Tiffany jewellery collection has achieved iconic status, particularly as a bracelet. The original logo – minus the registration number, which has been swapped for hallmarking numbers 925 for silver or 750 for 18ct gold – is now stamped across all manner of jewels, from signet rings and heart-shaped earrings to bold statement cuffs.

RIGHT:
A silver Return to Tiffany bracelet on display in a store window.

Jackie Bracelet

Jean Schlumberger's bright enamel bracelets were a huge hit for Tiffany & Co. in the 1960s; made all the more successful because of one very special patron. Jackie Kennedy, wife of President John F. Kennedy, was gifted her first Schlumberger bracelet by her husband in 1962 and would go on to collect many more, often wearing stacks at a time. She wore them so often that they became – and remain – known as the Jackie bracelet.

The gold bracelets, often accented with diamonds, are decorated in rich colours using a 19th-century enamelling technique known as paillonné. This is an incredibly intricate process that requires cutting complex shapes out of gold foil, placing them onto the bracelet and then dipping the entire jewel into translucent enamel in the required shade. This must then be repeated, as many as 60 times, to achieve the right look. Though Tiffany & Co. does offer the occasional Jackie bracelet for sale, those in search of a Jackie bracelet will often have more luck on the auction circuit or in the listings of upmarket vintage jewellery dealers.

LEFT:
A gold and enamel Tiffany & Co. Jackie bracelet, once owned by Lauren Bacall.

Bone Cuff

The Bone Cuff was created more than 50 years ago, yet it looks as fresh and provocative as when it first tripped off the sketch pad of Elsa Peretti in the 1970s. Inspiration for this sensual and ergonomic jewel, which is today crafted in copper, silver or gold, came from the Capuchin crypt in Rome. In this room beneath the 17th-century Santa Maria della Concezione del Cappuccini church, which is decorated with thousands of human bones, Peretti saw beauty in the darkness and wanted to create a cuff that celebrated the human form rather than constricted it.

The Bone Cuff has won many celebrity fans over the decades, from Liza Minelli to Margot Robbie, with stars often opting to wear one on each wrist. Such is its legend as a symbol of female empowerment that *Wonder Woman 1984* director Patty Jenkins insisted Gal Gadot's Diana Prince character should wear one during the film.

RIGHT:
An Elsa Peretti Bone Cuff, worn by Athena Calderone to the 2014 Tiffany & Co. Blue Book Gala in New York.

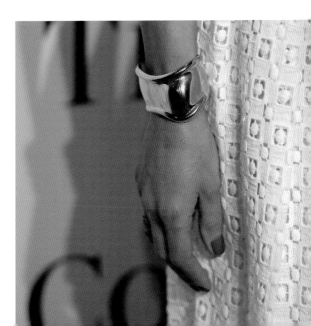

Diamonds by the Yard

Diamonds by the Yard is a simple concept, but one that has captivated shoppers at Tiffany & Co. for decades for its novel versatility. This was one of Elsa Peretti's first assignments when she joined Tiffany & Co. in 1974. Tasked with creating simple diamond jewellery for women on a budget, she devised a necklace with small diamonds in bezel settings spaced in uneven intervals along a simple chain. It is said it was her friend, the fashion designer Halston, who came up with the humorous name Diamonds by the Yard when he first saw her creation.

The name stuck and proved to lend itself well to the evolution of the collection, with the diamond-dotted chains cut to size for bracelets, earrings, necklaces and even rings. By altering the length and material of the chain and the number of diamonds, it not only caters to those on a budget but also those who want to amp up the luxury. The beauty of Diamonds by the Yard is in its simplicity. As Peretti once said: "What can I say about my jewellery? It speaks for itself. For me, style is to be simple."

LEFT: A model wears Diamonds by the Yard necklaces on the catwalk of a Reem Acra fashion show in New York in 2017.

Tiffany Keys

The first Tiffany Keys launched in 2009 and took inspiration from a lucky find in the archives. The design team had been looking back through the jeweller's extensive back catalogue and found a set of exquisitely crafted keys, the oldest of which dated back to the 1880s.

Struck by the beauty of elevating everyday objects, the designers created a collection of precious keys in gold and platinum, designed to be worn on a simple chain. The keys had elaborate heads inspired by antique ironwork and were set with diamonds and gems. Tiffany & Co. says the Keys symbolise "independence, power and optimism" and the unlocking of new possibilities. This sentiment has made the Keys, now also available in silver, a popular gift.

The Tiffany Keys collection has grown and evolved over the years with fresh motifs including fleurs-de-lis, trefoil knots, hearts, flowers and kaleidoscopes. There is even a brutally contemporary design that looks more like it might open a front door rather than a secret jewellery box.

RIGHT: Tiffany & Co. Key necklaces on display in a store window in Milan, Italy.

Tiffany T

One of the most instantly recognisable Tiffany & Co. jewels is the Tiffany T bangle, an open-ended cuff that presents as a curving, double-ended letter T. This cult classic was part of the Tiffany T collection created by Francesca Amfitheatrof in 2014. It was Amfitheatrof's first collection for the jeweller and she said at the time that she wanted to "create a symbol for modern life and the relentless energy that flows through New York". The minimalist design was also carried through to hoop earrings, rings and other jewels.

This was not the first time that the T motif had been used at Tiffany & Co.; for one, Tiffany creative director John Loring created a block motif T pattern for his collections in the 1980s. However, it captured the imagination of the fashion crowd. Tiffany T has continued to evolve and expand, with diamond-set accents or colourful gemstone inlay, and in 2021 designer Reed Krakoff offered up his spin on the T with the more geometric T1 collection.

RIGHT: Actress Lili Reinhart wearing a Tiffany T necklace at a Tiffany & Co. event in Los Angeles in 2019.

HardWear

Tiffany HardWear is not for the faint of heart. Inspired by the industrial cityscape of New York, this collection is defined by heavy gold or silver chains created using what the jeweller terms 'gauge' links – thick, glossy loops of metal tipped with spheres that interconnect. When creative director Francesca Amfitheatrof unveiled this collection in 2017 – her final for Tiffany & Co. – it was heralded by *Vogue* as signalling "the return of the statement piece". The collection was, in fact, inspired by a unisex chain bracelet decorated with a padlock and gold ball found in the jeweller's archives that dated back to 1971, a time when bold gold jewels were de rigueur.

HardWear has become a celebrity favourite, with the likes of Scarlett Johansson, Zoë Kravitz and Lady Gaga using it to bring a tough luxe edge to outfits. In 2021, K-pop idol Rosé from Blackpink made her debut as a Tiffany & Co. ambassador wearing jewels from the HardWear collection.

LEFT: Silvia D'Amico wears necklaces from the HardWear collection to a Tiffany & Co. dinner in Rome in 2017.

Creating Retail Theatre

As Holly Golightly explained in *Breakfast at Tiffany's*, there is something magical about walking into a Tiffany & Co. store. Whether you are there to buy a one-of-a-kind jewel or a silver trinket, Charles Lewis Tiffany decreed long ago that the experience must be just as enchanting.

More than just excellent customer service, the jeweller strives to bring an element of theatre to its shopping experience, through artistic and thought-provoking window displays, historic store locations and now the chance to actually have that breakfast at its stores. What started as a stationery store in 19th-century New York has expanded into a slick empire that spans the globe.

OPPOSITE: A creative festive window display at Tiffany & Co. on Bond Street, London.

A Retail Empire

Tiffany & Co.'s retail empire began at 259 Broadway. Charles Lewis Tiffany and his business partner plumped for a boutique on the tree-lined street in New York City, with the jeweller – then a stationer and fancy-goods purveyor – opening up shop in 1837, opposite the grand City Hall and its surrounding park.

New York would be the heartland of Tiffany & Co., with the jeweller later moving into its iconic current flagship on Fifth Avenue in 1940, but the US was just the start for this ambitious brand. Tiffany wanted his brand to be respected as an international jewellery player at a time when American brands were not revered. To stake his claim as an equal among the European maisons, Tiffany & Co. opened a boutique in Paris in 1850. As well as a signal of intent, it also served as a way to deliver jewels to loyal American clients travelling in Europe. Tiffany & Co. would continue to evolve its Parisian presence as brand awareness grew, culminating in a no-expenses-spared boutique on the city's chic and luxurious Place de l'Opera in 1910. Meanwhile, it had been building its British operations, opening a store on London shopping promenade Regent Street in 1891.

Despite these early international adventures, the real expansion of Tiffany & Co.'s retail empire began in the 1970s when the jeweller set its sights on Japan. Teaming with department store group Mitsukoshi, Tiffany & Co. mini boutiques started popping up within its stores. By the time Tiffany & Co. opened a flagship store in Tokyo's upscale shopping district Ginza, there were 38 of its boutiques in Mitsukoshi stores and the country was its largest market after the US.

The rest of the world would soon follow. Tiffany & Co. now operates more than 300 boutiques across the globe, including locations in Central and South America, Canada, Europe, the Middle East, Asia, India and Oceania. Its top market remains the US, where it has more than 90 stores, although Japan has remained an important outpost with 70 boutiques.

ABOVE: A Tiffany & Co. store in London.

A New York Institution

On the intersection of New York's Fifth Avenue and West 57th Street lies the spiritual home of Tiffany & Co. The famous corner store, whose windows were so beautifully captured by a pastry-eating Audrey Hepburn in *Breakfast at Tiffany's*, has magnetised thousands of shoppers each day since its opening in 1940. The building itself, a seven-storey structure designed by firm Cross & Cross, is an architectural marvel. Look around the 8,400sq ft ground floor, gleaming with freshly polished glass cabinets filled with treasures for sale, and you will notice something is missing: structural columns. To create a clean, open space, the architects delivered a feat of engineering to ensure the structures for the 24ft-high ceiling are hidden within the building.

Other architectural flourishes are easier to spot. The entrance, guarded by the iconic Atlas Clock, is adorned with the jeweller's signature wheat leaf pattern in a nod to Art Deco architecture. As well as a place to buy jewels or silverware, Tiffany & Co. has become a mecca for tourists who simply wish to step inside the famous store. The jeweller actively encourages this, seeking to attract guests with exhibitions, including the permanent display of the enormous Tiffany Diamond, as well as lavish window and store dressing – especially around Christmas, when the displays are legendary. You can also stop by for refreshments at the Blue Box Café.

The Fifth Avenue store closed its doors temporarily at the beginning of 2020 as it embarked on a two-year renovation plan – the building's first in its 80-year history – estimated to cost $250 million. Keeping the Tiffany & Co. magic alive in the interim, the jeweller opened a temporary

four-storey flagship next door, helpfully called Tiffany Flagship Next Door. This modern space served as a stop gap for Tiffany & Co. fans until the original 10-storey Art Nouveau flagship reopened.

ABOVE: A Tiffany & Co. store on Wall Street in New York.

I Do on Fifth Avenue

Nothing says romance like a Blue Box, but some couples have taken their passion for Tiffany & Co. further by choosing to propose in the famous Fifth Avenue store in New York. There have been both spontaneous droppings to one knee as well as pre-planned proposals requiring help from the sales team at Tiffany & Co.

Not only does the team encourage such on-brand displays of romance, they have also been known to throw in some extras, such as arranging celebratory dinners, clearing requested areas of the store for perfect proposals, and generally engaging in subterfuge to help nervous suitors achieve the element of surprise. Tiffany & Co. likes to refer to the purchase of one of its engagement rings as sparking "a lifetime of service". Rather than referring to upcoming marital duties, it speaks to the beginning of a life-long relationship between couple and jeweller.

As well as offering complementary cleaning and a diamond check every six months, it will also carry out any required repairs. Should you decide a few years down the line that your original rock was not quite big enough, Tiffany & Co. will allow you to trade in your original as part-exchange for something a little flashier.

In recent years, Tiffany & Co. has sought to cater to relationships of all kinds. It became the first major jewellery brand to feature a same-sex couple in an advert in 2015, has a line of genderless commitment rings and launched a collection of men's engagement rings in 2021.

RIGHT:
A model in a Reem Acra wedding dress wears Tiffany & Co. diamonds at a fashion show in New York in 2017.

BELOW:
Tiffany & Co. promotes its bridal offer at a store in Hong Kong.

The Atlas Clock

When Tiffany & Co. moved to 550 Broadway in 1853, Charles Lewis Tiffany assessed the building and declared its façade to be "monotonous". In order to bring more interest to his store, and therefore his jewels, the retailer commissioned his friend, the carver Henry Frederick Metzler, to create something special to be positioned above the doorway. Metzler, who mostly made figureheads for the bows of ships, created a 9ft-tall statue of Atlas, the figure from Greek mythology who is often pictured holding the world on his shoulders. The figure, which would hold up a clock rather than a globe, was carved in wood and painted to mimic patinaed bronze.

The Atlas Clock became part of the Tiffany & Co. legend, with its customers regularly using it to synchronise with 'Tiffany time' or test a 'New York minute'. When the store moved to its current location on Fifth Avenue, so too did the Atlas Clock. Such is its connection to the brand you will see replicas created to adorn its modern stores around the world. The clock has also inspired a jewellery and watch collection at Tiffany & Co.

PREVIOUS:
Decorations inspired by the Tiffany Diamond bring sparkle to Tiffany & Co.'s Fifth Avenue store in New York.

OPPOSITE:
A replica of the famous Atlas Clock outside a Tiffany & Co. store in Vancouver, Canada.

ABOVE:
An exterior
view of a
Tiffany &
Co. store in
Hong Kong.

TOP RIGHT:
The Tiffany
& Co. store
in the ION
Orchard mall
in Singapore.

BOTTOM
RIGHT:
Tiffany
& Co. on
Bond Street
in London.

OVERLEAF:
The stairs of
Los Angeles'
Rodeo Drive
are transformed
with Tiffany Blue.

TIFFANY & CO.

Iconic Window Displays

Gazing through the glass of a Tiffany & Co. store window is much like looking upon a theatre set, with glittering jewels in place of players. The jeweller has built a reputation for creating fantastical dreamscapes in miniature, each designed to lure passers-by into a whimsical world of fantasy.

The tradition started with Charles Lewis Tiffany himself. The King of Diamonds was no shrinking violet, and he recognised the marketing power of a provocative window display. One of his numerous gimmicks included a partnership with the legendary American showman P. T. Barnum.

In 1868, the marriage of two of Barnum's circus performers, the 2ft 11in General Tom Thumb and 2ft 7in Lavinia Warren Bump, proved to be a major society event in New York, with Barnum selling 5,000 tickets to the wedding reception at $75 each. Tiffany & Co. joined the hype by creating a bejewelled silver carriage, commissioned as a gift for the couple by Barnum, and displaying it in the window of its Broadway store, where it pulled in the crowds.

In the following century, Tiffany & Co. would forge a partnership that would elevate its store windows to legendary status with the arrival of Gene Moore in 1955. Moore had studied as an artist and dabbled in photography – he took the iconic black-and-white shot of Audrey Hepburn looking back over her shoulder. Moore would later

PREVIOUS:
A window
display at a
Tiffany & Co.
store in New
York.

OPPOSITE:
An architectural
scene in a store
window in
Milan.

BELOW: A
bracelet hangs
from the arm of
a figure riding
a moped at a
store in Milan.

"When someone looks into a Tiffany window, I want him or her to do a double – even a triple – take. I want him to experience the sudden fresh insight the Zen philosophers call the 'ahness'"

Gene Moore

LEFT:
A surrealist display at a Tiffany & Co pop-up in New York's West Village.

OPPOSITE:
Diamonds and cleaning products in a 2019 display in New York.

be reunited with Hepburn on the set of *Breakfast at Tiffany's*. His true calling, however, was visual merchandising.

A true visionary, his charming, witty and often radical displays pioneered a new form of art. Each scene had a narrative: tiny mannequins tussled over jewels, toy diggers extracted necklaces from sand pits, and floating hands pulled strings of pearls from takeaway cartons with chopsticks.

Moore would spend 39 years at Tiffany & Co., creating more than 5,000 window displays during that time. He also called on the talents of other artists. Jasper Johns, Andy Warhol and Robert Rauschenberg were among the creatives to lend their vision to Tiffany & Co. windows. The influence of his groundbreaking work is still evident in the creativity on display at Tiffany & Co. stores today.

Blue Box Café

If there is one thing that everyone wants to do at Tiffany & Co., other than buy diamonds, it is to have breakfast à la Holly Golightly. That fantasy became a reality in 2017 with the opening of the first Blue Box Café on the fourth floor of its New York flagship store.

With fresh white linen and Tiffany & Co. china, accented with Tiffany Blue, of course, guests can sit down to a breakfast far heartier than Golightly's coffee and croissant – champagne is optional. Or should an early rise not be on the cards, perhaps a lavish afternoon tea with sandwiches and cakes, including Tiffany & Co.-inspired desserts.

The first Blue Box Café was an instant success, drawing daily queues with its first-come-first-served policy. The concept soon spread. Cafés opened at stores in Tokyo's Harajuku and Shanghai's Hong Kong Plaza in 2019, as well as a Beverly Hills pop-up that same year. In 2020, another opened in London department store Harrods, followed by South Coast Plaza in Costa Mesa, California, in 2022.

RIGHT: A Tiffany & Co.-branded coffee cup from an in-store café.

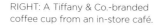

ABOVE:
Zizi Donohoe
and Stephanie
Liu Hjelmeseth
at the Blue Box
Café pop-up at
Beverly Hills
in 2019.

RIGHT:
A place setting
laid out with
Tiffany & Co.
tableware at the
2019 Blue Box
Café pop-up in
Beverly Hills.

Salesroom Sensation

A combination of great craftsmanship, top-quality gemstones and a signature household name tends to signal success at jewellery auctions. As such, Tiffany & Co. pieces often do well on the secondary market. This is particularly true for rare or one-off pieces, as well as jewels that can be linked to famous names.

One of the most expensive pieces of Tiffany & Co. jewellery ever put up for auction was a platinum and gold ring gifted to Shirley Temple by her father George Temple in 1940, to celebrate the 12-year-old actor filming *The Blue Bird*. The ring, which was set with an extraordinarily rare 9.54ct fancy blue diamond, had a pre-sale estimate of $25 million to $35 million when listed at Sotheby's in 2016. The piece, however, failed to sell and was later bought by antiques dealer Windsor Jewelers, which broke the ring apart so it could recut the diamond.

More successful sales at Sotheby's included a Tiffany & Co. necklace set with an 18.44ct internally flawless diamond, which sold for HK$14 million in 2021, and a platinum Tiffany Setting engagement ring with a 13.47ct diamond that sold for more than HK$12 million in the same sale. That same year at Sotheby's, a gold, opal and garnet Medusa necklace designed in 1904 by Louis Comfort Tiffany, son of the brand's founder, sold for more than $3.5 million.

Another notable sale took place at Christies in 2001, when a platinum ring set with a 62.02ct blue sapphire known as the Rockefeller Sapphire, having once been owned by American financier John D. Rockefeller Jr, achieved a final price of more than $3 million when the gavel fell. In 2021, Tiffany & Co. caused a stir in the watch world when it teamed up

with long-time collaborator Patek Philippe to create a signed Tiffany Blue dial for one of its Nautilus 5711 watches. This quirky creation was put up for auction at Phillips in New York and sold for $5.35 million. All the proceeds were donated to charity Nature Conservancy.

Beyond Jewels

Dazzling diamonds might be the first thing that springs to mind when you think of Tiffany & Co., but the American luxury brand has built a lifestyle empire that is so much more than just jewellery.

From its very beginnings as a purveyor of fancy goods, the jeweller was the place to buy luxurious homewares and silver gifts. It still is, although its repertoire has grown far beyond that now. Whether a perfume, handbag, watch or pair of sunglasses, Tiffany & Co. has lent its design nous and its iconic Tiffany Blue to a whole range of accessories.

OPPOSITE: A silver Tiffany & Co. watering can engraved with a sunflower motif.

Homeware

In the 19th century, the height of elegance for any American homemaker was to have a table adorned with silverware crafted by Tiffany & Co. This was the era of silver flatware, hollowware and dishes; everything from the serving spoon and platter to the coffee jug and candelabra would have been made in solid silver in the most upmarket homes.

Though expensive, hefty and in need of constant polishing, such pieces would prove to be good investments. Tiffany & Co. silver homeware often comes up at auction, prized not just for its use of precious metal but also its craftsmanship and design heritage. In 2018 at auction house Sotheby's, a pair of Tiffany & Co. silver pitchers from 1883, decorated with elephants and botanical patterns, sold for $68,750 and a set of cutlery sold for $30,000.

As tastes in homeware moved on, Tiffany & Co. focused on creating china tableware sets that soon became just as coveted as its silver. In 1968, funded by an anonymous donation, Tiffany & Co. designed a 2208-piece china set for the White House at the request of First Lady Claudia 'Lady Bird' Johnson, wife of President Lyndon Johnson. The set was decorated with American wildflowers and cost $80,000.

Homewares remain an important part of Tiffany & Co. today. Shoppers can accessorise their homes with dinner sets, barware, photo frames and all manner of trinkets and decorative items that bear the stamp of the American luxury brand. For those with deeper pockets, many of its

OPPOSITE: Tiffany & Co. ceramic jewellery trays within a window display at a store in Moscow, Russia.

designs are available in solid silver, as a nod to its heritage, but its makers also work with glass, porcelain and leather. Dinnerware sets that feature the famous Tiffany Blue are particularly popular. Tiffany & Co.'s jewellery designers have long influenced its homewares, and some of the most popular designs in the home section were created by Elsa Peretti, whose signature sensuality transfers well to

items such as glasses, carafes, letter openers and bowls. Particularly coveted is her Thumbprint collection, which gently indents the rims of glasses and bowls as if she has pressed her thumb onto them.

ABOVE: A Tiffany & Co. china tea set in the window of a store in Brussels, Belgium.

Watches

Though jewels have always been its first love, Tiffany & Co. has a long history of selling watches. It first started to sell timepieces at its New York store in 1847 and a few years later it established a collaboration with a young horological upstart in Geneva – Patek Philippe.

Now considered to be one of the world's greatest, and most exclusive, watchmakers, Patek Philippe was established just two years after Tiffany & Co. and the two companies felt an affinity. Tiffany & Co. became the watchmaker's established retail route into the United States, while Patek Philippe would make movements for the jeweller's own-brand watches.

It was the popularisation of pocket watches that spurred Tiffany & Co. to develop its own collections and it opened a watch factory on Geneva's Place Cornavin in 1874 to handle the manufacture. A speciality was gold pocket watches, which were also sold to other retailers. Tiffany & Co. later sold this operation to Patek Philippe. Notable moments in Tiffany & Co.'s watchmaking history include winning a prize at the 1889 Exposition Universelle in Paris for a floral brooch designed by Paulding Farnham that had a small watch dial set within a bloom.

In 1903, its chief gemmologist George Frederick Kunz invented a luminous (and radioactive) paint that made numerals glow in low lights – similar safer substances are widely used in sports watches today.

In the early 20th century, miniaturisation of watch movements led to the creation of sought-after bejewelled

Art Deco dress watches for ladies. Then in 1945, Tiffany & Co. gifted a gold calendar watch to US President Franklin D. Roosevelt on his birthday, which he wore to meet Winston Churchill and Joseph Stalin at the Yalta Conference of World War II allies that year.

In the mid 20th century, Tiffany & Co.'s watch production faltered and it has failed to become a serious player. It does, however, still produce a limited run of watches, including collections inspired by Roosevelt's watch, the Art Deco cocktail timepieces and the Atlas Clock that sits above the entrance to its Fifth Avenue store. It also continues to collaborate with Patek Philippe, with models bearing the American jeweller's branding on the dials selling for tens of thousands – and even millions – of dollars.

Accessories

By the 21st century, Tiffany & Co. was a global superpower and, as such, the jeweller sought to capitalise on its brand equity. Following in the footsteps of luxury fashion houses, it sought to create a line of accessories that would capture the spirit of the brand.

In 2008, Tiffany & Co. signed a licensing deal with Italian eyewear maker Luxottica Group, which produces the iconic Ray-Ban sunglasses. The two companies had high hopes for the collaboration, with Luxottica forecasting that the sunglasses and reading glasses it would produce under the jeweller's branding could generate as much as €50 million a year. The union proved to be a success, with the glasses selling well at both Tiffany & Co. stores as well as through Luxottica's network of more than 11,000 boutiques across the world. The styles often feature flashes of the iconic Tiffany Blue, while the shapes take inspiration from the brand's jewellery collections. During his tenure as chief artistic officer at Tiffany & Co., Reed Krakoff designed a special collection, marking the designer's first foray into eyewear.

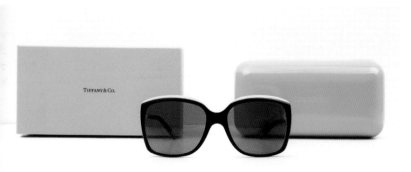

In 2010, Tiffany & Co. launched a collection of bags at its stores, each featuring Tiffany Blue either in the lining or on a clasp. The range catered to men and women, with prices ranging from $395 for a suede tote bag to $17,500 for a large crocodile handbag. The current leather range at Tiffany & Co. is more modest, with plain leather bags bearing its branding stamped onto them. It has also created a wider range of leather goods, from luggage tags to trolley bags.

You can also pick up a trinket for your pet at Tiffany & Co. The jeweller has a range of accessories for upmarket furry companions that includes Tiffany Blue leather collars adorned with the iconic Return to Tiffany metal plate and solid silver food bowls. Should human company be more your thing, there are myriad Tiffany & Co.-branded gifts within the accessories department, from pens, keyrings and cufflinks to more unusual poker kits, petanque balls and solid silver golf tees.

RIGHT:
Bags and purses from Tiffany & Co.'s leather goods range.

OPPOSITE:
A pair of branded Tiffany & Co. sunglasses with Tiffany Blue box.

Fragrance

In the late 1980s, Tiffany & Co. decided to take the brand in a new creative direction and launched its own fragrance. The jeweller teamed up with perfumer François Demachy, who would later become head of fragrances at Dior, to create a floral scent for women called Tiffany.

The scent was sold in major department stores across the United States in 1987, allowing fans of the brand to buy into Tiffany & Co. in a new way. Two years later, the jeweller commissioned Jaques Polge, who was at the time head perfumer at Chanel, to create a corresponding men's perfume. In 1995 a new fragrance was launched – a floral fruity scent with woody undertones titled Trueste, however, it was later discontinued.

In 2017, Tiffany & Co. took a fresh crack at developing its fragrance offer. New bottle shapes were devised that took inspiration from the jeweller's most famous diamonds, including the Tiffany Diamond and the exclusive 50-facet

square-shaped Lucida diamond cut it launched in 1999. The Tiffany line remained in production, and the house added a new perfume to the line-up, masterminded by Daniela Andrier, who has created scents for many fashion houses including Kenzo, Giorgio Armani and Miu Miu. Simply titled Eau de Parfum, the subtle floral musk was designed to offer an olfactory equivalent of slipping jewellery onto bare skin. The jeweller followed this up in 2019 with two launches: Sheer, which it describes as the "aromatic equivalent of a diamond", and his 'n' hers line Tiffany & Love. Rose Gold followed in 2021 with notes of blackcurrant and lychee fruit.

When Tiffany & Co. opened two new concept stores in London's Covent Garden and Kings Cross in 2018, it installed vending machines stocked with its perfumes, allowing shoppers to pay and go using contactless payments.

RIGHT:
A vending machine selling Tiffany & Co. perfume in London.

OPPOSITE:
Tiffany & Co. perfume on sale at a store in Shanghai.

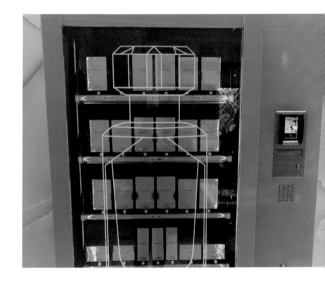

Continuing the Legacy

Tiffany & Co. has a rich history that spans three centuries, but all great brands know that too much looking back can stunt future growth.

With an eye on the future, the American jeweller, which is now owned by luxury group LVMH, has been revamping its public image to attract a younger clientele, with strategic celebrity partnerships and quirky publicity stunts. It has also been working to address the concerns of a new generation of jewellery fans by making supply chain transparency a key selling point of its diamonds while also giving back to nature.

OPPOSITE: A decorative window at a Tiffany & Co. store in Rome.

Tiffany for a New Generation

For fans of Tiffany & Co. it has been clear to see that the American jeweller has been undergoing somewhat of a direction change over the past few years. Under the leadership of chief artistic officer Reed Krakoff, the messaging shifted from proposals over candlelit dinners to diamonds matched with Tiffany Blue hoodies.

In 2018, Tiffany & Co. delivered a contemporary reboot to one of its most famous brand associations – *Breakfast at Tiffany's*. In homage to Audrey Hepburn's smooth crooning of *Moon River* in the film, actress Elle Fanning and rapper A$AP Rocky were drafted in to create a cover for a new Tiffany & Co. ad campaign. Fanning starts with a decent, stripped-back impression of Hepburn, then the beat drops and A$AP Rocky begins with the line, "I ain't window shopping today". He later raps about "Tiffany grills with the all gold filling" and references the Tiffany T Square ring, a "canary on the finger" presumably in reference to a yellow diamond like the famous Tiffany Diamond, and plays out a lyrical fantasy of having breakfast at the jeweller.

The song played over a short film that had Fanning recreating the iconic start of the 1961 film, with the actress staring in the windows of

TIFFANY & CO.

There's Only One CAMERON RUSSELL

the Fifth Avenue flagship, filmed in black and white, before exploding into bright colour with dancers in all manner of Tiffany Blue outfits, from firemen to feisty-looking school girls. It was a signal of intent: yes, this is a brand with a famous heritage, but it can surprise you, too.

Another musical partnership geared to shifting the perception of Tiffany & Co. was with Lady Gaga, who the brand teamed up with to air its first ever Superbowl commercial in 2017. Since then, the jeweller has used one of her songs – *Is That Alright?* written for film *A Star Is Born* – as the background to an engagement ring advert and dressed the pop icon in its jewels at numerous red carpets, including the 2019 Oscars at which she wore the Tiffany Diamond.

Beyoncé and Jay-Z are two more celebrities lending their fame and influence to the jeweller, creating a short film titled *About Love* that was released in 2021. Shot by director Emmanuel Adjei, the film shows the couple in a luxurious Los Angeles house, decorated with artworks by Jean Michel Basquiat. Beyoncé, dressed in the style of Hepburn's Holly Golightly character, sings her own version of *Moon River* over the top. In the film and print advertising, Beyoncé wears the Tiffany Diamond, making her only the fourth woman in history to do so. Jay-Z also wore accessories by the jeweller, including a gold and diamond Apollo brooch, one of Jean Schlumberger's iconic designs, pinned to the lapel of his tuxedo.

Other interesting collaborations include asking provocative artist Daniel Arsham in 2021 to reimagine its Blue Box in his Future Relics aesthetics; he created a limited series of 49 bronze sculptures that showed a decaying, eroded box with crystal structures growing out of it.

As well as positioning itself with leaders of influence, Tiffany & Co. has also been trying to change the way it speaks to customers in its marketing. In 2015, it became one of the first major luxury jewellery houses to run an ad for commitment rings targeted at same-sex couples. It has since flexed its bridal jewellery offering to cater to all types of relationships, with a line of engagement rings for men and a curation of couple's rings to replace the traditional mix of wedding bands and an engagement ring with two matching – or not – bands.

For anyone not picking up on the subtleties of its efforts to appeal to a new generation, Tiffany & Co. quite literally spelled out its intentions with a 2021 ad campaign featuring the tagline: Not Your Mother's Tiffany.

OPPOSITE: Pharrell Williams arrives at a Kenzo fashion show in 2022 wearing a pair of diamond sunglasses he created in collaboration with Tiffany & Co.

Cleaning up Diamonds

Historically, diamonds have not enjoyed the most glittering of reputations when it comes to ethics. They have long been associated – fairly or unfairly – with human rights abuses, negative environmental impact, war zones and murky backroom deals. When Charles Lewis Tiffany was at the helm, such tales had little impact on the sale of his jewels, but in the modern era consumers have many questions when it comes to how and where diamonds have been mined.

As such, the diamond industry has been cleaning up its act, and Tiffany & Co. has been at the forefront of much of that change. In 2006, it became one of the founding members of the Initiative for Responsible Mining Assurance (IRMA), which seeks to offer consumers confidence through third-party auditing of mining operations. It is also fully audited and certified by industry watchdog the Responsible Jewellery Council (RJC).

While many luxury jewellers have preferred the code of silence that keeps the sourcing of precious elements mysterious, Tiffany & Co. has been unafraid to step into the limelight when it comes to sustainability. In 1995, it campaigned against the opening of a gold mine that would encroach on Yellowstone National Park, despite sourcing most of its gold in the US, and in 1999 it pushed the US to adhere to the Kimberley Process that sought to eliminate conflict diamonds. Over the years, it has also boycotted Burmese rubies due to human rights atrocities in Myanmar, and coral due to environmental concerns. In 2011, it joined the United Nations Global Compact, committing to improve its sustainability credentials, and in 2015 pledged to achieve net-zero greenhouse gas emissions by 2050.

Such efforts have not gone unnoticed. When activist group Human Rights Watch (HRW) launched an investigation into the jewellery industry in 2018, titled *The Hidden Cost of Jewellery*, the American jeweller came out on top. While none of the organisations it scrutinised were deemed to be 'excellent', and therefore fulfilling all the criteria for responsible sourcing, Tiffany & Co. was the only company to win recognition on the next tier 'strong', in recognition of taking significant steps in the right direction. It was a position it maintained when HRW launched a follow-up investigation in 2020.

Yet more strides are in the pipeline. In a document titled 2025 Sustainability Goals, the jeweller, which does not own or operate any mines, outlined its ambitions to achieve 100 percent traceability for all its precious metals and

ABOVE: A gemmologist checks a diamond for imperfections.

individually registered diamonds (stones of at least 0.18ct). It has already achieved the latter by becoming the first global luxury jeweller to provide customers with provenance information on all of its diamonds through its Diamond Source Initiative. To keep track of the gems, a serial number is etched onto each diamond, which is imperceptible to the naked eye, and this can unlock information on where the diamond was sourced, as well as its journey from rough to polished gem.

The metal holding the diamonds is also under review. In 2021, Tiffany & Co. made its first purchase of Fairmined gold and has pledged to increase its use of artisanal gold mines to represent 5 percent of its gold supply by 2025, while increasing the amount of recycled gold it uses to 50 percent of total supply.

Even those iconic little Blue Boxes holding its diamonds are getting a sustainable overhaul. The materials required to create them are 100 percent ethically sourced, it says, with 50 percent of the materials coming from recycled sources.

In 2022, Tiffany & Co. publicly pledged to pause buying diamonds from major Russian diamond producer Alrosa, which is majority owned by the country's government. The company produces more than a quarter of the world's diamonds.

OPPOSITE: Diamonds are coming under ever-increasing scrutiny as consumers prioritise ethics.

Giving Back

Like most heritage global brands, Tiffany & Co. has a philanthropic arm; one that funnels millions of dollars each year into causes that are close to its heart. The environment is one such passion, and in particular responsible mining practices and coral conservation projects. Since 2000 the Tiffany & Co. Foundation has awarded more than $90 million to non-profit organisations that seek to advance these two causes.

One such organisation is Trout Unlimited, a charity that has been working to restore abandoned mine sites in the United States by reinstating rivers and rejuvenating natural habitats so that wild trout and salmon can thrive. Tiffany & Co. has also made $6 million in grants available to support the creation of responsible mining standards and development opportunities for the artisanal mining sector.

As well as supporting conservation efforts at coral reefs in more than 30 countries, which has led to the preservation

RIGHT:
Tiffany & Co.
has committed
to funding the
preservation
of coral reefs.

of more than 10 million km² of ocean, it has also funded educational films about coral reef conservation, including the Netflix documentary *Chasing Coral*.

Tiffany & Co. also has a legacy of donating to community projects and non-profit organisations in the cities it operates in, with its corporate contributions hitting nearly $20 million in 2020. Another focal point is championing diversity initiatives and female empowerment, both through support of external and internal activities.

Much of this local-level philanthropic work is led by its employees, and this is something the jeweller encourages through employee resource groups that can set agendas and decide where donations should be allocated. It also runs a scheme called Tiffany Cares that fosters a philanthropic mindset among staff by donating $20 for every hour its staff volunteer at charities, as well as matching employees' fundraising efforts up to $1,000 a year for every member of staff.

RIGHT:
Louis Comfort Tiffany was a great supporter of The Metropolitan Museum of Art in New York.

A New Owner

The beginning of 2021 ushered in a new era for Tiffany & Co. when the American jeweller was bought by French luxury conglomerate LVMH for $15.8 billion – its most expensive acquisition to date.

LVMH already owns a number of watch and jewellery houses, including Chaumet, Bulgari, TAG Heuer, Zenith and Hublot, as well as fashion houses that produce jewellery such as Dior and Louis Vuitton. It was a rocky road to the sale, with LVMH and Tiffany & Co. publicly spatting in a legal dispute as the luxury group sought to lower the price it would pay. This is not the first time that Tiffany & Co. has been owned by a corporate entity. In 1978, the business was – disastrously – sold to cosmetics company Avon, which led to a fall in sales and reputation. Within five years, the business was back on the market and an investment group would make it a public company once again.

The full impact of the LVMH sale on the historic jewellery brand is yet to be felt, but early changes included a management reshuffle, involving the exit of chief artistic director Reed Krakoff, and an official statement claiming that "the potential ahead is limitless".

OPPOSITE: A Louis Vuitton store in Kyiv, Ukraine, in 2017.

A New Diamond

One of the most impactful things that Charles Lewis Tiffany did to assure the trajectory of his brand was to purchase an important diamond – the 128.54ct yellow Tiffany Diamond. Now, seeking to forge a new chapter in its history, the brand has once again secured a historic gem.

The Empire Diamond, named for the Empire State Building in New York, is an oval-shaped 80ct flawless white diamond, which was cut from a larger rough stone discovered at a mine in Botswana. It has been set in a platinum necklace, along with 578 additional smaller diamonds, the design of which was inspired by a necklace that Tiffany & Co. made to exhibit at the 1939 New York World's Fair. The necklace was designed to be transformable – a key element of many high-jewellery pieces. In this instance, the Empire Diamond can be detached and worn as a ring, with a platinum and diamond-encrusted setting.

The necklace was unveiled as part of the Blue Book 2021 collection. While the jeweller won't reveal the price of the gem – although experts have pitched guesses at about $20 million – it is said to be the most expensive piece of jewellery ever to be sold by Tiffany & Co. With an estimated value of $30 million, the Tiffany Diamond trumps it, of course, but that jewel, still proudly on display at its Fifth Avenue home, is not for sale.

OPPOSITE: Lady Gaga wears the historic Tiffany Diamond, the company's first iconic purchase and most expensive jewel.

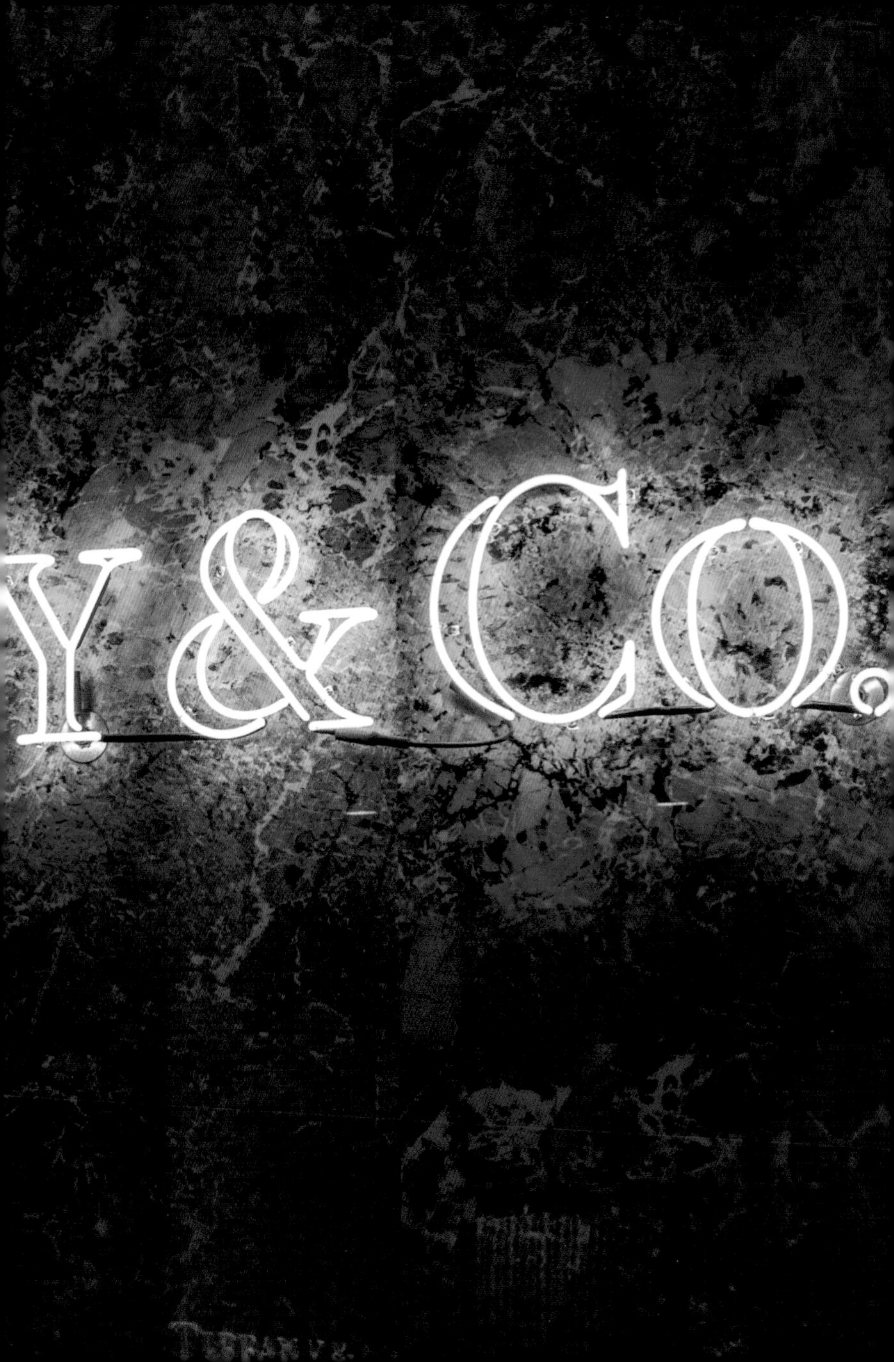
Y & CO.

Image Credits

OPPOSITE: A Tiffany & Co. window display in Barcelona dressed for the holiday shopping season featuring a Return to Tiffany necklace.